Our Stories

TEN POUND POM

Carole Wilkinson
& Liz Anelli

Atlantic Ocean
SHEFFIELD
DERBY
TILBURY
English Channel
BAY of BISCAY
ITALY
SPAIN
NAPLES
GIBRALTAR
Mediterranean Sea
PORT SAID
Lake Timsah
SUEZ CANAL
AFRICA
EGYPT
ARABIA
Red Sea
ADEN
Equator
N
Indian Ocean

CEYLON
COLOMBO
Pacific Ocean
Equator
AUSTRALIA
PERTH
Fremantle
ADELAIDE
Great Australian Bight

CHILD
3453
ORIENT

I don't want to go to Australia. I have just started grammar school. My best friend Sally goes there too. We're learning Latin and French.

Two weeks ago, my family and I put on our best clothes and caught a train to Birmingham, where a man asked us questions to make sure we'll be good migrants. Dad was nervous. Mum answered most of the questions. I was hoping she'd get the answers wrong, but I could see what the man wrote on our application:

Quite a nice family.

Dad has always wanted to live in Australia, ever since he was a boy. When he married Mum, she didn't want to emigrate and leave her family. Then in 1962 there was something called the Cuban missile crisis, and it looked like there could be another world war, only this time it would involve nuclear bombs. Dad has finally convinced Mum to go to Australia.

I have a collection of cards about Australia that came in tea packets. In Australia, there are artesian wells, corroborees and coolibah trees. There are spiny anteaters, black swans and sharks.

Today a letter came to say we have been accepted. We are leaving in March. That's only six weeks away. It's a long way to Australia. I don't think we'll ever come back to England.

Dad makes two big wooden boxes and we pack our belongings into them:

the dining table

my bike

Mum's sewing machine

Dad's tools

my brother Brian's train set

all of our plates and saucepans

I carefully wrap my collection of 101 glass animals in tissue paper. But I'm not allowed to take my teddy bear.

"We all have to leave something behind," Mum says. "Anyway, you're too old for a teddy bear."

I want a souvenir of England to take with me. I have a small aspirin bottle. I'm going to fill it with soil from the garden – English soil.

It's March, but there's still snow on the ground. Dad says it's been the coldest winter on record. I find a trowel and try to dig the soil; it's frozen solid. I get a garden fork from the shed. But no matter how hard I try, I can't dig up any soil. Not a crumb.

I fill the bottle with snow instead. Just before Dad nails the lids on the boxes, I slip the bottle between some pillow cases. Men from the shipping company come and take the boxes away. There is nothing left in the house. I write a poem about an empty house.

Uncle Steve picks us up. Our neighbours come out to say goodbye and wish us luck. I can see Sally up at the corner. She waves goodbye and then goes off to catch the bus to school, as if it's any other day. Through the back window of the car, I watch the neighbours going back into their houses.

We drive to Grandma and Granddad's to say goodbye.

"I'll never see you again," Grandma says to me.

She won't come to the railway station to see us off. Granddad has already gone to work.

At the Derby railway station, my aunt and uncle come to say goodbye. Mum's cousin is there with her new baby. At the last minute Granddad arrives on his bike. He's managed to get an hour off work. He gives Mum a hug.

"Don't worry about your Mam and me," he says.

Mum has to wipe her eyes on her hanky.

I don't cry, even when we pull out of the station and Derby slips into the distance. We pass through Spondon and Borrowash, Market Harborough and Flitwick. I'll probably never see those places again.

The train takes us to Tilbury Docks. And there at the wharf is our ship – the SS *Arcadia*. It's big, taller than any building in Derby.

CADIA
CONDITIONS AND RE
By accepting or using this Ticke
ORIENTAL STEA
subject to the c
he covers contain
Ship
Bert
ICKET
oyage
shipowner may at its option
made available and
all periods when Shipow

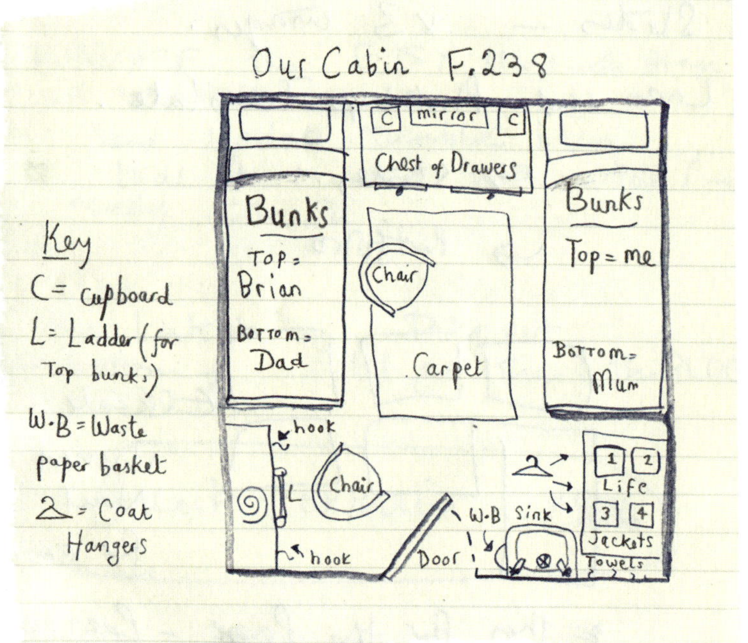

We struggle up the gangplank with our suitcases.

Our cabin is on F Deck. Because we're migrants, the voyage is costing Mum and Dad only £10 each. Brian and I travel for free. Dad says that's why we're on the bottom deck. The cabin has two bunk beds, a chest of drawers, two chairs and a sink. Brian and I get to sleep in the top bunks. We don't have a porthole. Our cabin is under the sea.

At 6 pm, tugboats pull the *Arcadia* away from the wharf. There are lots of people waving goodbye and throwing paper streamers. All the passengers are leaning on the rails. Some of them manage to catch the ends of the streamers. I wish I had a streamer to hold on to, but no one is here to wave goodbye to us. The streamers pull tighter and tighter until they break.

The next morning we pass Beachy Head.
It looks cold and grey.

"Say goodbye to England," Dad says.

Mum doesn't say anything.

Then we are out of the English Channel and into the Bay of Biscay. The sea is rough. The wind is icy.

The waves get bigger and bigger. I feel ill. The ship rocks so much it's hard to stand up in the corridors. I am sick in our cabin sink. I can't eat. There's nowhere to get away from the rolling and rocking. Brian comes down to tell me we're sailing past the coast of Spain, but I'm too sick to get up and have a look.

Then we sail into the Mediterranean. The sea changes from grey to blue. The ship stops rocking and I don't feel sick. I manage to eat a little tomato soup and some ice-cream. I have a shower for the first time. At home, we had only a bath. None of the migrants have passports, only travel permits. We aren't allowed to get off when the ship berths at Gibraltar.

The *Arcadia* is like a huge floating hotel. We have a cabin steward called Alvarez who wakes us in the morning with tea and biscuits. At home, we had dinner at midday and tea at six. On the ship we have four meals a day – breakfast, lunch, tea and dinner. Every meal has at least three courses. My appetite returns. I've never eaten so much in my life. Crew members fill the swimming pool and I unpack my shorts. In the evenings we watch films, and people dance to a band called the Arcadians.

The sun shines every day. Brian makes friends with two boys. They sneak into the First Class section where we aren't supposed to go. I explore the ship on my own. There are nine decks. I count the number of steps from F Deck all the way up to the Promenade Deck. There are 84.

I play draughts with Dad in the Games Room or sit on deck and read. Mum takes part in the deck quoits competition. I'm allowed to buy a Coca Cola. I've never tasted it before.

There is a girl about my age that I see in the dining room. I smile at her but she doesn't smile back.

The coast of Italy comes into sight. After tea we dock at Naples, and I stand on foreign soil for the first time. We go into the town. Mum buys a little musical table that plays "Isle of Capri". I buy a doll in traditional Neapolitan dress.

Back on the *Arcadia*, we have our dinner – soup with letters of the alphabet in it, roast duck with liver stuffing and chocolate gateau. After dinner Italian singers come on board to entertain us.

Every morning Alvarez brings us a newsletter, which tells us the day's activities, the ship's longitude and latitude, and if there is anything we will be able to see. It also tells us how far we've sailed. We are already 2296 miles from England.

We've sailed right across the Mediterranean. Dad wakes me at midnight so I can see Port Said. Small boats come alongside us, and Egyptian men throw ropes to passengers so that they can haul up baskets of souvenirs for sale. I buy a stuffed leather camel at three o'clock in the morning!

I sleep for a little while, then get up again at 6 am, as we are sailing down the Suez Canal. It's strange to have land so close on both sides of the ship after seeing nothing but sea.

On one side is Arabia and on the other Egypt. Mostly they are both just sand; occasionally there are palm trees, and men in long robes. I see some camels.

We have to stop in Lake Timsah to let a convoy of ships pass us going the other way.

After dinner, a conjurer called a gulli-gulli man comes on board. He is very good. He produces little yellow chicks from everywhere, including one from Mum's blouse!

We are now in the Red Sea. It is hot, 72 degrees Fahrenheit (22 degrees Celsius).

I am allowed to stay up when there is a film showing at the cinema. Tonight there is *Dr No* starring Sean Connery as James Bond. Brian plays with his friends. Mum gets into the finals of the ladies quoits competition. I don't have much to do. I take Brian to the children's lunch and dinner. I go in the swimming pool, but it gets very crowded. I write a letter to Sally. I wonder what she's doing. I don't know what time it is in England because every few days we put our watches forward half an hour.

Dad is fed up with me moping around.

"Why don't you go to that teenagers' pop music session this afternoon?"

"I'm only twelve and three-quarters," I say. "I'm not a teenager."

"That's close enough."

When I get to the Starboard Gallery, it's full of dancing teenagers who are all older than me. The girl I've seen is also there. I sit next to her. Her name is Jennifer and she comes from Sheffield. Like me she used to listen to Radio Luxembourg when she was at home, under the blankets at night, the signal fading in and out. It's good to hear pop music again, but we are too shy to dance.

Today we arrived at Aden, which is somewhere in Arabia. We can't pull up to the wharf, so stairs are lowered from C Deck and we climb into a small boat that takes us ashore. As well as souvenirs there are electrical goods for sale. Dad buys me a portable record player and transistor radio combined. I buy a Cliff Richard LP to play on it.

When I unpack the record player back on the ship, I find it doesn't have batteries. Jennifer is very keen to hear my record. She gets her dad to buy batteries from the ship's shop. We spend the afternoon in our cabin playing Cliff Richard four times. We do the Twist. It's fun.

This is the third time that Jennifer's family has immigrated to Australia. The first time was before she was born, and they went to live in Sydney. Her mother was homesick and missed her family. They went back to England when Jennifer was still a baby. But her mum had forgotten how cold it was. The second time, they immigrated to Melbourne when Jennifer was six. That time her dad couldn't get a job and they were stuck in the migrant hostel. For three years they lived in something called a Nissen hut, which was like a cylinder of corrugated iron that had been cut in half, so they went back to England again. Now they are going to Perth. Jennifer's dad says this time they're staying.

We won't have to live in a migrant hostel. We're going to stay with my aunt and uncle until we get a house of our own.

Today it was 84 degrees Fahrenheit (28.9 degrees Celsius). We're sailing through the Indian Ocean. Jennifer and I sunbake on the Promenade Deck and take part in the deck sports competition. I win the balloon race. My prize is a purse shaped like a sailor's hat. We see dolphins and flying fish. Tomorrow we'll dock at Ceylon. Dad was there for three years during World War II.

Jennifer and I arrange to meet at 5 am so we can watch the ship dock at Colombo. Hardly anyone else is on deck. We pretend we are famous actresses on our own private ship.

I go on a bus tour with my family. We visit a temple where there is a statue of Buddha lying down. It is 24 feet (7.3 metres) long and painted bright colours. We stop at a beautiful beach fringed with palm trees. Tiny crabs scuttle across the sand. I paddle in the sea and it's as warm as a bath.

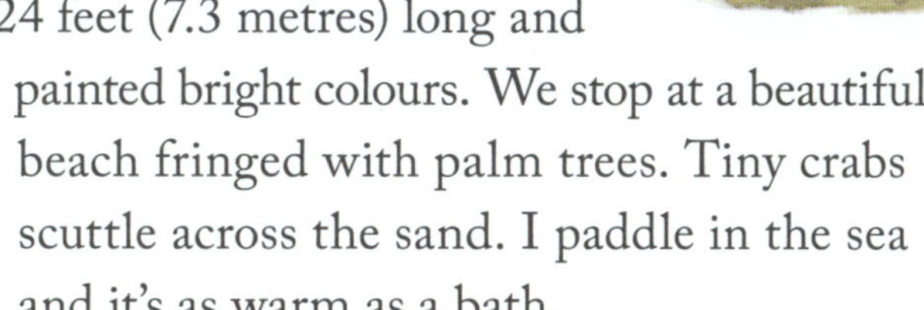

Back on the ship, after dinner, we are entertained by traditional dancers and a snake charmer.

We cross the equator. Jennifer and I take part in the Crossing the Line Ceremony. King Neptune takes over the ship (it was one of the crew dressed up). We are squirted with tomato sauce, lime juice and have ice-cream smeared all over us. Then we are dunked in the pool. We are 7238 miles from England.

We have been in the Indian Ocean for a week. Around us there is nothing but sea. Jennifer and I play draughts and Scrabble. We watch cartoons with the children, then listen to pop music in the Verandah Cafe. This time we pluck up the courage to dance.

We make costumes for the Fancy Dress Ball. I wear a cardboard box and go as a packet of sugar. Jennifer's dad goes as a big baby wearing only a sheet done up like a nappy and carrying a baby's bottle. Jennifer pushes him in a wheelchair. They win a prize.

We arrive at Fremantle. It's our first sight of Australia, which is exciting.

I also have to say goodbye to Jennifer, which is sad. I write my aunty's address on the back of a postcard of the *Arcadia* so that we can be penfriends.

We go on a bus tour of Perth. After seeing foreign places, Australia looks more British, but it is also different. There are a lot of gum trees. Everyone lives in bungalows. And there really are black swans, just like on my tea cards. It's cooler than I expected. Dad says that even though it's spring in England, in Australia it's autumn.

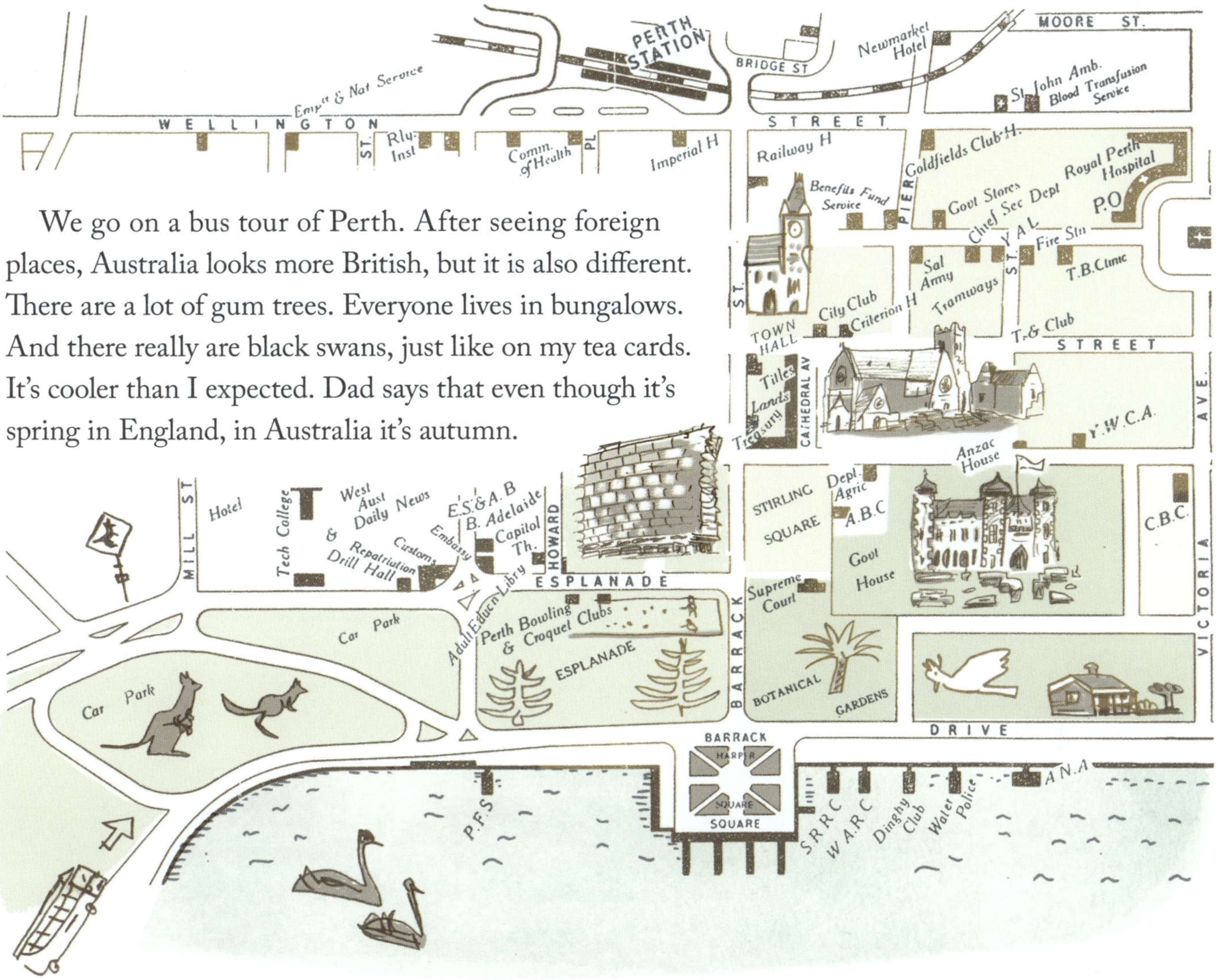

The sea is rough as we cross the Great Australian Bight and I feel a bit seasick again. Alvarez brings a note with our tea and biscuits. The boxes with all our belongings in them are not on board. They were accidentally left behind.

When we wake up, the ship has already docked in Adelaide. Brian and I rush up on deck. There are crowds of people waiting on the wharf. We have sailed 11,397 miles, lost eight and a half hours and skipped summer. I find Aunty Peg in the crowd. My uncle and two cousins are there too. We wave at them.

We walk down the gangplank for the last time. It takes ages to go through customs as there are a lot of migrants disembarking in Adelaide. We are reunited with our relatives. It's been five years since they immigrated. They're all very brown and cheerful. My cousins have grown.

It's going to be crowded in their three-bedroom bungalow.

It's four months since we arrived in Adelaide. Mum and Dad have bought a house in an outer suburb near the beach. No one has lived here before, except perhaps Aboriginal people. We are like pioneers.

There are drop-tail lizards

redback spiders

and the occasional snake.

Also plants with thorns called three-cornered jacks.

Our house is brand new. It is triple-fronted, cream brick with a laundry, a breakfast bar and stencilled patterns on the walls. The bathroom is pink and grey and has a glass shower screen with a shark and a treasure chest etched onto it. There is a drive-in movie theatre around the corner. Three radio stations play pop music all day. We buy our first ever car and fridge.

Our missing boxes finally arrive. Dad levers off the lids and there are all our belongings. We have lunch sitting at our own dining table. I unpack my glass animals. None of them broke.

I find the medicine bottle that I hid among the pillow cases and unscrew the lid. It's empty. I knew the snow would melt, but I wasn't expecting it to have evaporated as well. I don't feel upset.

In England my pocket money was two shillings and sixpence each week. Now I get 10 shillings. I have my own room again. I go to the beach with my cousin Ivan, who walks all the way there without any shoes. I collect pretty shells and sea urchins.

Perhaps living in Australia won't be so bad.

The £10 Migration Scheme

At the end of World War II, Australia's population was only 7 million. Australia had been threatened during the war. Singapore had fallen to the Japanese. Darwin had been bombed. Australia's long coastline was largely undefended. Members of the Australian government thought that invasion was still possible.

At the same time, Australian industry was thriving. If it was to continue to grow, more workers were needed. There was one thing that would solve both these problems – immigration.

"We must fill this country or we will lose it," said Arthur Calwell, the Minister for Immigration.

Calwell envisaged the country populated by a particular kind of migrant, what he called "people of our own British stock". He wanted ten migrants from Britain for every "foreign" migrant.

In Britain there was concern that migration would take all the nation's skilled workers. These people were needed to rebuild post-war Britain. On the other hand, Australia was a member of the British Commonwealth and so it was inevitable that the people that settled there were British. To encourage British people to immigrate, the British and Australian governments came up with a scheme of assisted passage. **The United Kingdom–Australia Free and Assisted Passage Agreements started in 1947.** Ex-servicemen who wanted to immigrate could travel to Australia for free. Other adults paid only £10, and children under 18 came free. In Australia, British migrants became known as "Ten Pound Poms".

Assisted passage for British migrants was nothing new. Australia had always seen itself as a British country. Between 1860 and 1919, 45 per cent of all British migrants arriving in Australia were assisted by the Australian government. However, with this new scheme the British government contributed too, helping to pay for their own people to leave.

Immediately after the war, people in Britain were still living with food rationing. The Australian government enticed migrants with the promise of sunshine and plentiful food – especially meat. People signed up to immigrate. And just like the earlier British settlers, they came by sea.

Calwell's dream of 10:1 migrants being British was unrealistic, and the goal was lowered to 50 per cent British migrants. The foreigners or "aliens" that Australia was trying to limit were people from Europe, such as Italians, Greeks, the Dutch. The White Australia Policy prevented people from Asian and African countries settling in Australia.

British migrants had special privileges. They could become Australian citizens after just one year. Migrants from Europe had to wait five years. Britons could vote in Australia, even if they didn't take out citizenship. There was only one condition on their immigration: if they returned to England in less than two years, they had to repay the full price of their outwards voyage.

Few people who emigrated were poverty stricken or unemployed. They were looking for a better standard of living. They wanted to own their own homes. They wanted to be able to afford a car. In the 1960s, worries about another war became another factor that made people emigrate. But it was still a big decision to leave home and family behind for a life 12,000 miles away on the other side of the world.

Early participants in the scheme travelled on ships converted from troop carriers. By the 1960s, migrants sailed on cruise ships, experiencing the same comforts and entertainments as full-fare paying passengers. Unlike early migrants who sailed to Australia, the voyage was not an ordeal to be endured; it was like a month-long, all-you-can-eat holiday. An experience never to be forgotten.

More than one and a half million Britons immigrated to Australia

between 1945 and 1982. Around 20 per cent of them returned to Britain after two years.

During the 1960s, more and more British migrants came by air. Then in 1973, Britain joined the European Economic Community. Australia lost its position as Britain's most favoured trading partner to European countries.

Australian businesses turned to Asia. Japan, no longer feared as an enemy, took Britain's place as Australia's major trading partner. Australia found itself in the embarrassing position of forbidding people from its most important trading partners to immigrate. The White Australia Policy was abolished. British migrants lost their special privileges and were subject to the same conditions as all migrants. **In 1982, the assisted migrant scheme ended.**

Arcadia Facts

Built in 1954 by John Brown & Co, Clydebank
as a passenger ship for **£6,664,000**

Full speed
Powered by
6x turbine engines,
23 knots

Dimensions
721 ft (**219** m) **long**
90 ft (**27** m) **wide**
40 ft (**12** m) **depth**

Cargo
4560 tons of **oil** for fuel, burned at a rate of
230 tons per day at a cost of £10 per day

1754 tons of fresh **water**,
280 tons consumed every day

400 tons of **stores**

1000 tons of **refrigerated** cargo

2000 tons of **other** cargo

Displacement
32,632 tons

Tonnage
29,664

Passengers
1392
657 first class
735 tourist class

Crew
678

Broken up for scrap metal in 1979 in Taiwan

Glossary

artesian well • A bore drilled deep into the Earth to reach reservoirs of fresh water trapped underground. In Australia, bores are drilled into the Great Artesian Basin, a huge body of water that is up to 3000 metres deep and covers an area of 1.7 million square kilometres. It reaches from the northern tip of Queensland into South Australia, the Northern Territory and New South Wales.

bungalow • A single-storey house. In Britain, most houses are two storeys. There aren't many single-storey houses and British people call them bungalows.

Ceylon • Now known as Sri Lanka.

coolibah tree • A type of eucalyptus tree that grows near rivers and creeks.

corroboree • A gathering of Aboriginal tribes, usually involving singing and dancing.

Cuban missile crisis • In October 1962, the US government discovered that the Soviet Union was building nuclear missile bases in Cuba, just a few hundred kilometres from the US coast. It led to a war of words between the two superpowers. At the time people were afraid it would lead to World War III.

displacement • A measurement of the volume of water that is displaced or moved by a ship floating in the sea.

emigrate • To leave a country to go and live in a different country.

equator • An imaginary line around the middle of the Earth, at an equal distance from the North and South Poles.

European Economic Community • An organisation, formed in 1958, which aimed to bring together the financial systems of European countries. It later became part of the European Union.

immigrate • To come to a country to live there permanently.

knot • A unit of speed used for ships and aircraft, equal to one nautical mile per hour.

LP • Short for "long-playing". It was used as a short name for vinyl records that contained an album of songs.

Poms • An Australian nickname for English people.

pound (£) • The currency of the United Kingdom. Today, £1 equals around $1.60 Australian.

Radio Luxembourg • An English-language radio station that broadcast from Luxembourg, in Europe, to the UK. In the 1960s, the radio station broadcast mainly pop music. In Britain, the only other radio station that played pop music was the BBC Light Programme, where pop records were permitted to be played for just a few hours per week.

sea urchins • Sea creatures that live inside spiky round shells.

starboard • The right-hand side of a ship when standing facing the bow (front).

tonnage • The total volume of space in a ship that is available for cargo, fuel, passengers and crew.

White Australia Policy • The popular name for various Australian federal government policies that prevented Asians, Polynesians and other non-white people from immigrating to Australia between 1901 and 1973.

Index

For Brian. CW

For those who've come across the seas. LA

First published in 2017 by black dog books, an imprint of Walker Books Australia Pty Ltd
Locked Bag 22, Newtown, NSW 2042 Australia
www.walkerbooks.com.au

National Library of Australia
Cataloguing-in-Publication entry:
Ten pound pom / Carole Wilkinson;
illustrator, Liz Anelli.
ISBN: 978 1 925381 21 4 (hardback)
Series: Our stories.
Subjects: Wilkinson, Carole, 1950–
Immigrant children – Australia – Biography
Immigrants – Australia – Biography.
British – Australia – Biography.
Assisted emigration – Australia – 20th century.
Other Creators/Contributors: Anelli, Liz, illustrator.

The illustrations for this book were created with mixed media

Typeset in Adobe Caslon and Agenda
Printed and bound in China

Images from the P&O Heritage Collection and images bearing P&O Trademarks reproduced by kind permission of P&O Heritage Collection.
Page 21: Perth map reproduced with kind permission of Tourism Western Australia.
Page 29: Ten-pound fare poster, 1962: National Archives of Australia: A12111, 2/1962/34A/1.

The author, illustrator and publisher thank P&O Heritage for their expert help in researching this book.